Sir Francis Drake and the Spanish Armada 1588

Arthur L. Clamp

Artist's impression New Street which runs down to the Barbican. It was built by John Sparke in 1584 and was certainly known to Drake.

This combined version of two shorter books is virtually as originally published, one after the other. There are now additional pages at the back providing information about the author.

The republishing project is being managed by Arthur's grandson, Steven Gibson. We aim to find all the research that he was involved in publishing, preserving it for the next generation as part of 'The Clamp Collection'.

FRANCIS DRAKE (c1543-1596)

There have been many famous people born in the large county of Devon and one of the most well known must be Drake through whose daring exploits during the Elizabethan years he became a national hero. Like many others of his stature he came from a relatively humble background and through good fortune, determination and much courage, some say foolhardiness, he defeated the might of the Spanish navy and caused havoc across their lines of shipping with the Americas.

He was the eldest son of a yeoman farmer born close to Tavistock about fifteen miles north of Plymouth. They had to flee to Kent in 1549 through the troubles of the Prayer Book rebellion and it was there that he first went to sea as an apprentice to the master of a small coasting vessel. During the 1550s he successfully pursued his interest in the sea undertaking voyages to Guinea and gaining much experience in the art of seamanship and command over men.

He came to the attention of one of Queen Elizabeth's ministers, William Cecil, after having narrowly escaping being captured by the Spaniards while on a slave-trading expedition with his kinsman, John Hawkins of Plymouth, in the West Indies. He was then in command of the 50 ton *Judith* but managed to get the ship away and return to Plymouth. This was in 1569, the year in which he married a local girl, Mary Newman, in the parish church of St. Budeaux, then just northwest of Plymouth.

His first encounter with the Spanish prompted him to find out by what route the gold and silver from Peru was brought back to Spain and for this he spent the years 1570-71 finding out as much as possible about the town of Nombre de Dios on the isthmus of Panama. With two small ships and 73 men he left Plymouth on 24th May, 1572, to attack and capture this vital port on the Spanish Main. He was very successful in the surprise attack and found to his amazement a stack of 360 tons of silver, gold and jewels, more than the two ships could carry. However, through an injury and loss of blood he fainted and was carried back to his ship without any treasure.

Recovering from his wound, Drake remained in the area in the hope of finding out when the next Spanish treasure fleet was to leave Nombre de Dios. Two of his brothers and many of the crew died through fever during the year. However, in February, 1573, with only 18 men from the ships and 30 indians he made a daring and successful attempt at walking across the isthmus and becoming the first Englishman to sight the large Pacific ocean.

Luck was with him for on the return journey he laid ambush about a mile out from the town to a mule train carrying treasure to the port. They took as much gold as they could carry, burying the remainder, and making their way back to the ship. They eventually found them and returned to Plymouth triumphant in August, 1573, with about £40,000 of booty which would be worth millions today. It was on this return to Plymouth that the congregation of St. Andrew's Church left during the service to join thousands of other people flocking to the Hoe to see the two small ships come into harbour.

This achievement not only made him a rich man but brought him to the notice of the court and to the Queen when he related his adventures to her. Now he had the support and financial backing of many important people and was able to embark on his famous voyage of the circumnavigation of the world.

He brought together a squadron of five ships and 160 men with himself as Admiral in the *Pelican*. They left Plymouth on 13th December, 1577, and made for the Cape Verde islands where plans of his voyage were made known to all the crews. Trouble arose in them at the prospect of the long and uncertain voyage and a possible mutiny was quelled by the execution of Thomas Doughty on Drake's orders. Two of the smaller ships were abandoned and the *Pelican* was renamed the *Golden Hinde*.

The three ships sailed through the Straits of Magellan emerging into the Pacific where they were caught in a violent storm lasting 52 days. The *Marigold* was lost with all hands, the *Elizabeth* eventually made her way back through the straits to England and the gallant *Golden Hinde* was left on her own to continue this epic voyage.

The storm abated and Drake made his way northward in search of treasure ships. The Spaniards had assumed they were in full control of these waters and so did not arm their ships. The *Golden Hinde* captured one in March, 1579, taking so much gold, silver and chests of money that they could hardly stow all the loot. It was then not advisable to return to England by the way they had come so he planned to make his way across the Pacific and Indian oceans, round the Cape of Good Hope and so back to England.

Before this very long part of the journey he sailed northwards to what is now San Francisco where he refitted the ship out and claimed the land for the Queen as New Albion. In July, 1579, he started the long journey homewards and after many hazards and months of sailing finally made the port of Plymouth a very rich man indeed and the first, with his crew, to sail around the world. For this he was knighted by the Queen on his own ship at Deptford.

Now there was a five year break in his voyages during which he became Mayor of Plymouth, 1582, Member of Parliament, 1584, then the new owner of Buckland Abbey, planner of the Drake's leat, and a leading figure in the land. The period was marred by his wife dying but within a short time he remarried to a Elizabeth Sydenham in 1585.

The Queen commissioned Drake's next expedition in 1585 to the West Indies in answer to the embargo placed on English ships sailing in Spanish waters. Drake raided Vigo, San Domingo and Cartagena and brought home the English settlers in Virginia.

Preparations for war by Spain could no longer be ignored by the English. Drake was appointed to take charge of a strong squadron of ships and attack the Spanish fleet in their home waters. He reached Cadiz in April, 1587, where he sank or burnt 33 ships and captured others. This exploit is known as *the singeing of the King's beard* and delayed the sailing of the Spanish Armada for one year.

His other main achievement was the defeat of the Armada in 1588 details of which are covered in another part of this booklet. His game of bowls on Plymouth Hoe while the fleet was sailing up channel added to his image and defiance of the larger Spanish navy.

Drake was not without his bad luck and misfortunes the largest, perhaps, being the proposed invasion of Spain and Portugal in 1589. This was not successful and resulted in heavy losses among the 23,000 soldiers embarked.

His last voyage was to the West Indies again on the command of the Queen. He left Plymouth in August, 1595, and reached Puerto Rico in November in the hope of capturing the large amount of treasure known to be amassed there. He found the defences much stronger than he expected and much better organised. In spite of many attempted attacks he made no progress so he started to return but worn out from the effects of dysentery, he died aboard his ship on 28th January, 1596, and he was buried at sea.

A more suitable place to die and be buried could not have arisen for Drake whose long life had been so entwined with the sea and the call of adventure across the mighty oceans.

THE ARMS OF DRAKE

These were granted to Drake in 1581 by Queen Elizabeth I for his services to the country. The shield is symbolising the two hemispheres with the world encompassed. The ship at the top is guided around the globe by the Divine hand of Providence, *Auxilio Divino*. Below is the open visor indicating his rank. The lower inscription, Great Achievements from Small Beginnings, *Sic Parvis Magna*, summarises Drake's lifestyle and ambitions.

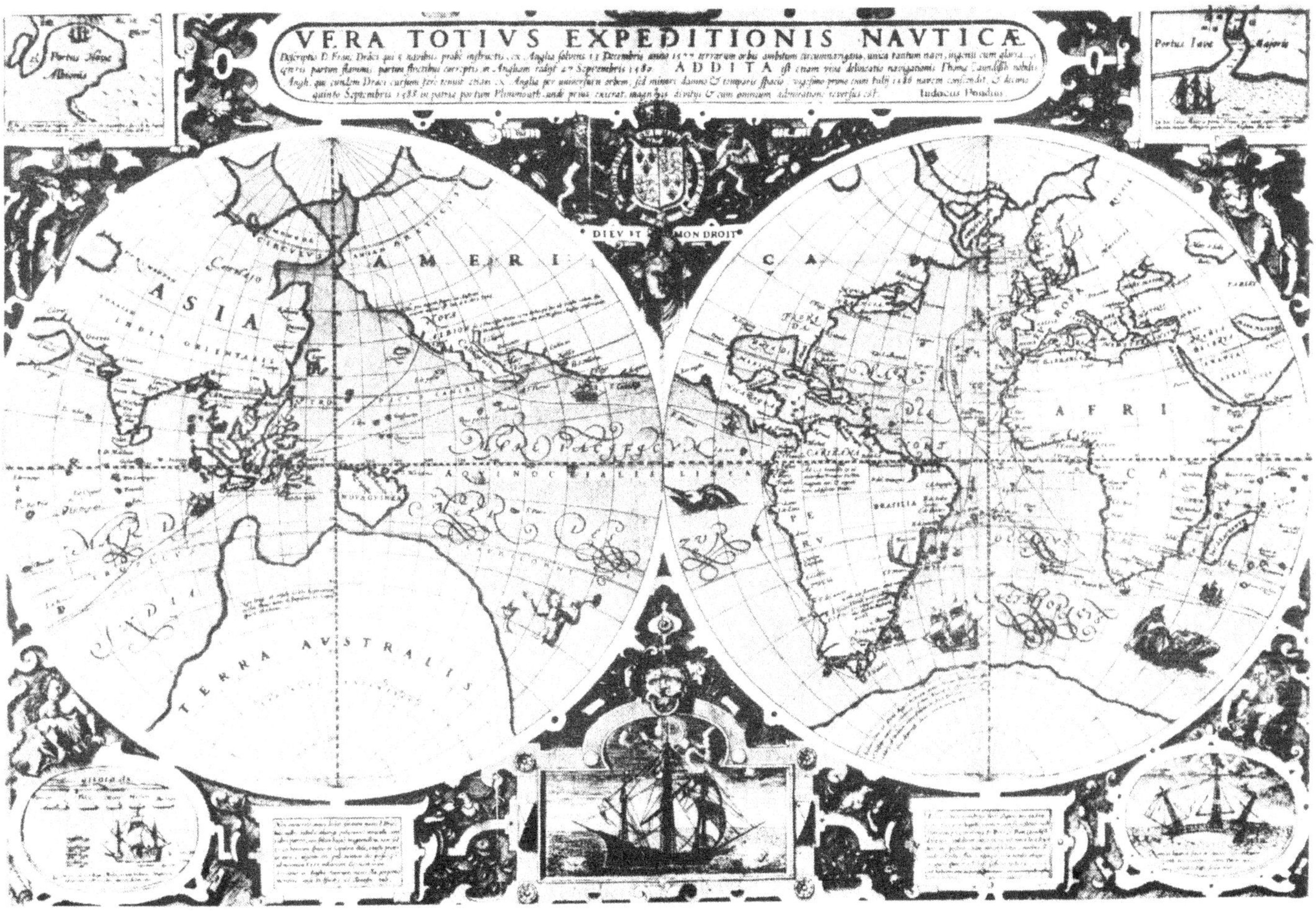

SHIP'S ENGAGEMENT

The *Golden Hinde*, to the right, is engaging a Spanish treasure ship somewhere near the Americas from which Drake made part his fortune.

THE GOLDEN HINDE AGROUND

The ship is seen here trapped by winds on the coast of Celebes. It had ran aground on a reef but by off-loading much cargo she was later freed and continued her journey.

REPLICA OF THE GOLDEN HINDE

As part of the 400th celebrations of Drake's circumnavigation of the world from 1577 to 1580 this very fine replica of his ship was built by J. Hinks and Sons, Appledore, North Devon, to plans painstakingly researched by an American naval architect, Christian Norgaard of California. There were no original plans. Ships of the 1500s were constructed more by eye than plan but after three years of research the resulting fine ship can be judged to be as near to the original *Golden Hinde* as possible.

The project was initiated by an American from San Francisco, Albert Elledge, and many craftsmen were engaged in making rigging, carving figureheads, etc. as they were once undertaken. Following the launch it came to Plymouth and was moored at the Mayflower Steps for a week then sailed to London where it was on view up until its crossing to San Francisco in September. It carried a crew of between 15 and 20 under the captaincy of Adrian Smell. Her projected sailing time was 142 days and she is now open to view close to the area where Drake claimed the land for the King as *Nova Albion*.

ST. BUDEAUX CHURCH

Francis Drake was married to Mary Newman on 4th July, 1569, in this church which is on the north side of Plymouth. The marriage entry is shown below.

SIR FRANCIS DRAKE'S SWORD

This sword was used by Queen Elizabeth I to confer the knighthood on Drake in 1581. Engraved on the blade are the Royal Arms and those of Drake. It was used by Queen Elizabeth II for the same purpose in 1967 when she knighted Francis Chichester after his solo voyage around the world in Gypsy Moth II.

DRAKE'S COCONUT CUP

This unusual cup, together with the sword, are kept in the Wardroom of H.M.S. Drake, Devonport. The arms of Drake are engraved on the coconut with the Royal emblems.

DRAKE'S SEAL

This is made of ivory and silver and contains the Drake coat of arms with the inscription, *the arms given to Sir Francis Drake for his voyage round the worlde by the Queen's Matie Anno Do. 1580.*

COMMEMORATIVE MEDALLION

This displays the *Golden Hinde* ship and was cast to commemorate the 400th anniversary of Drake's landing on the coast of California on 17th June, 1577.

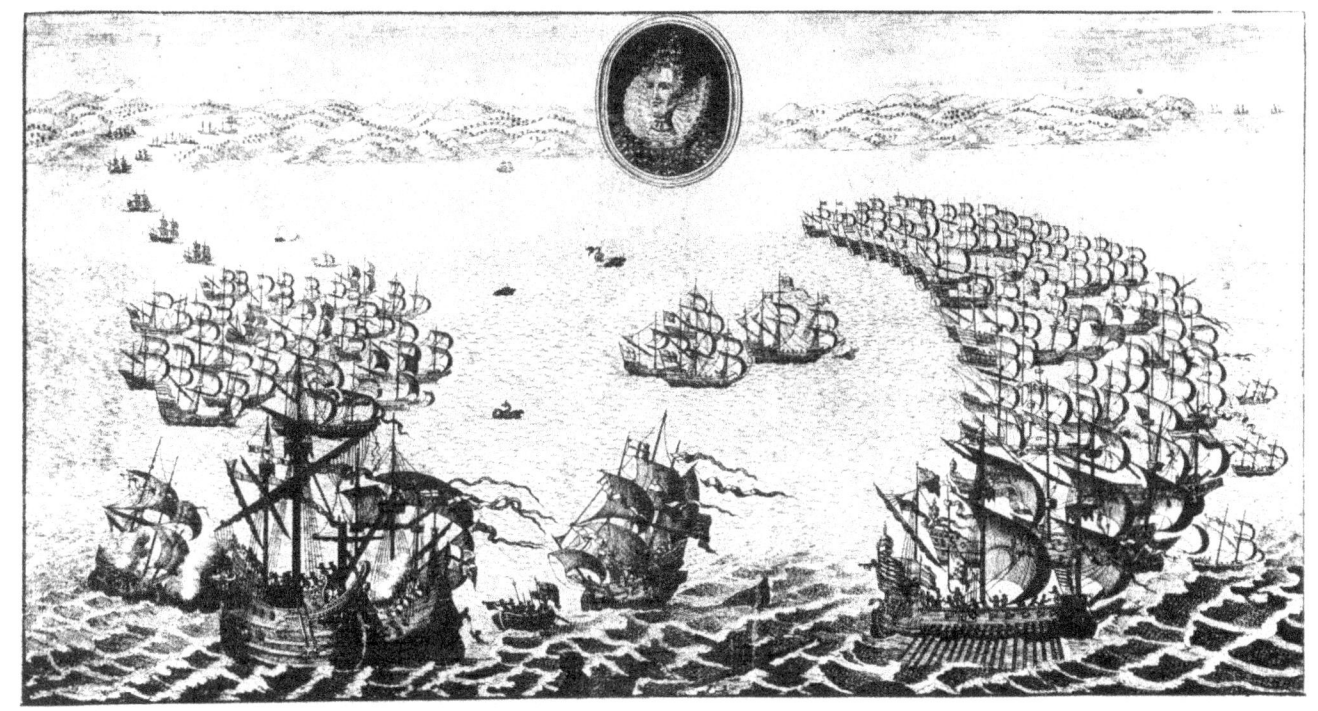

ILLUSTRATIONS OF THE ARMADA BATTLE

The above illustration, in tapestry, shows the English fleet in pursuit of the much larger Armada up the English Channel. In the lower one confusion appears to reign in a very close engagement between many ships further up Channel. Fireships would sometimes be sent in amongst the opposing fleet causing havoc and fire to the wooden vessels.

THE SPANISH ARMADA

Armada is a Spanish word meaning *armed force* which was a very appropriate title for the large Spanish fleet which assembled in Lisbon in April, 1588. Its purpose was to settle a political problem in the Netherlands and, more important, to restore the Roman Catholic faith in this country by military force.

The background to this move goes back some years before the 1580s. Spain was prospering through her conquests; she had conquered Portugal in 1580, and was as well equipped as any nation to undertake a variety of expansionist programmes. The idea of raising the Armada was first put forward in 1583 but its preparations had been delayed by Drake after his attack on the Spanish fleet at Cadiz in 1587. Philip II of Spain was an ambitious man and prudence was sometimes cast aside for risk and opportunity. The Armada scheme was vast by any comparisons with estimated costs around three and a half million ducats. The final costs in terms of lost ships and supplies must have been nearer ten million ducats which almost made the country bankrupt.

In spite of many difficulties and high running costs, the plans went ahead in the hope that the Armada would link up with the Duke of Parma's troops in Holland and that the English catholics would rise up in sufficient numbers to give support to the Spanish landings and the subsequent restoration of the Catholic faith throughout England.

The Armada was under the command of the Duke of Medina-Sidonia, a man who had little experience of the sea. He proved, however, competent although hamstrung by orders from Philip II. The Spanish fleet totalled about 130 ships including 20 powerful galleons, 4 galleasses, 40 armed merchantmen, all supported by a variety of pinnaces and supply ships. The ships were manned by over 7,000 sailors, carried about 19,000 soldiers, equipped with 2,000 cannon, and had in store enough food for six months. It was certainly a formidable force!

The Armada left home port and entered the English Channel on 29th July forming a crescent shape of its ships with the large galleons at the two ends of the crescent. This presented an almost impenetrable mass to the English ships.

The English fleet, under the command of the Lord Admiral Charles Howard of Effingham supported by Francis Drake and Sir John Hawkins, had far fewer ships of the first line than the Spaniards. The English ships adopted different tactics to those of the Spanish. They relied more on speed and flexibility and the power of their guns.

The Armada sailed slowly up the English channel having been spotted off Cornwall and reported to Drake during the playing of his famous games of bowls on Plymouth Hoe.

The Armada soon passed Plymouth where the English fleet was in readiness and the commander aware of the prevailing south-west wind which would soon take the smaller English ships up Channel in pursuance of the heavier and larger Spanish ships. The first skirmishes between the two fleets occurred off Portland Bill on 2nd August and off the Isle of Wight on 4th August.

Two days later the Spanish fleet anchored off Calais where the Duke of Medina-Sidonia had to wait for plans to link up with the Duke of Parma's troops in Holland. This was the opportunity the English admirals were waiting for. During the night of 7th August fire ships were sent in amongst the Spanish ships where great havoc was caused in the darkness and, by the morning, many of the ships had been scattered leaving the flag-ship, the *San Martin*, bearing the brunt of an attack from the surrounding English ships.

Although only 4 Spanish ships were lost in the encounter, many had been separated and riddled with shot. A sudden gale had arisen which carried many of the ships up the east coast of England towards Scotland and eventually past Ireland. The weather further deteriorated and the scattered Spanish fleet suffered very large losses 64 of the ships out of the original 130 getting back to their home port.

The defeat of the Armada was a turning point in the fortunes of Spain and the Habsburgs in Europe. The battle at Gravelines, off Calais, was described as, *Wonderful, great and strong,* and the intervention of Providence, through the storm, was hailed as a great sign by contemporaries. The words *God blew with his winds and they were scattered* appeared on a Dutch medal and is also on the Armada statue on the Hoe. It was very opportune for the English fleet to see their opponents scattered by the gale but it must not be overlooked that the new tactics used by the lighter English ships were to last as long as sail was in use.

Spain suffered a great loss through this episode in her history but she was still a power to contend with some years later. Her exploits in the Americas and the steady return of her ships laden with silver and precious stones enabled her even to consider another Armada in 1597. The threat of another invasion was finally removed when King James I made peace early in his reign.

Commemorative Medal
This was struck to mark the victory of this historic battle on which ships are shown and high winds with a running sea.

ARMADA MEMORIAL

This stands on the Hoe and was unveiled by H.R.H. Duke of Edinburgh on 21st October, 1890, to commemorate the defeat of the Spanish Armada in 1588. It was across the sea beyond the Breakwater that the Armada made its way up channel later pursued by Drake with the English fleet that set out from Plymouth.

SET OF ARMADA PLAYING CARDS

Many events and commemorative items were produced to celebrate the defeat of the Spanish navy including a set of playing cards depicting various stages of the battle. They were produced in 1590 and six of them are shown on this page. It was a novel way of making known the victory when the majority of people could not read or write but probably played card games.

The Prayer used at the time of the Armada
In time of Warre

O Almighty God, King of all Kings
and Governor of all things
whose power no creature is able to resist,
to whom it belongeth swiftly to punish sinners
and be merciful to them that truly repent;
save and deliver us (we humbly beseech Thee)
from the hands of our enemies, abate their pride,
assuage their malice and confound their devices:
that we being armed with Thy defence may be
preserved evermore from all perils,
to glorify Thee which art the only giver of all vitality;
through the mercies of Thy only son Jesus Christ our Lord.

NEW STREET

This narrow cobbled road was new in 1584, built by John Sparke, linking the Barbican wharf with the town. The fine merchant houses date from the same prosperous years and must have been familiar to Drake and his crew as they made their way from the berthed ships to the town or to St. Andrew's Church.

ST. ANDREW'S CHURCH

This is the Mother Church of Plymouth and it was within its thick walls that many famous men gave thanks for a safe return from their adventures or who asked for a blessing when they were about to leave port. Much of the building was erected after 1439 when Plymouth was granted its charter. The above illustration comes from the early 1800s and differs little from the time of Drake. On the return to Plymouth from one of his exploits it is recorded that the news was whispered from person to person during a service and the people left in haste leaving the preacher talking to an almost empty church!

THE DRAKE SCRATCHING

On the ledge of the window by the south door is a rough sketch cut into the plaster which is thought to represent the crest of arms granted to Drake in 1581. The drawing below came to light during restoration work and is thought to date from the sixteenth century. Drake's achievement and his return to Plymouth on 3rd November, 1580, must have created a great deal of interest out of which this scratching may well have arisen.

BUCKLAND ABBEY

This large thirteenth century Cistercian Abbey standing nine miles north of Plymouth was purchased by Sir Francis Drake from Sir Richard Grenville in 1581. It was Drake's principal property and remained in the Drake family for a remarkably long period of time until 1946. It was then acquired by the National Trust, leased to the city of Plymouth, and has been open to the public since 1951. It is certainly well worth visiting as it contains many items associated with Drake including his famous drum. It has had a chequered career but has been tastefully restored to the period. There are many exhibits of country crafts and also a very large tithe barn to see set in large grounds. The three illustrations below show two close ups of the Armada memorial on the Hoe and the nameplate of Plymouth's wide and spacious Armada Way.

THE QUEEN AND DRAKE

These four portraits show Elizabeth I and Drake regaled in their finery and remembered as such. The plate records the 400th anniversary of Drake's voyage and is in front of the statue of him on the Hoe.

DRAKE'S DRUM
By Sir Henry Newbolt

Drake he's in his hammock an' a thousand mile away,
   (Capten, art tha sleepin' there below?)
Slung atween the round shot in Nombre Dios Bay,
   An' dreaming' arl the time o' Plymouth Hoe.
Yarnder lumes the Island, yarnder lie the ships,
   Wi' sailor lads a dancin' heel-an-toe,
An' the shore-lights flashing', an' the night-tide dashin',
   He sees et arl so plainly as he saw et long ago.

Drake he was a Devon man, an' ruled the Devon seas,
   (Capten, art tha sleepin' there below?)
Rovin' tho' his death fell, he went wi' heart at ease,
   An' dreamin' arl the time o' Plymouth Hoe.
"Take my drum to England, hang et by the shore,
   Strike et when your powder's runnin' low;
If the Dons sight Devon, I'll quit the port o' Heaven,
   An' drum them up the channel as we drummed them long ago."

Drake he's in his hammock till the great Armadas come,
   (Capten, art tha sleepin' there below?)
Slung atween the round shot, listenin' for the drum,
   An' dreamin' arl the time o' Plymouth Hoe.
Call him on the deep sea, call him up the Sound,
   Call him when ye sail to meet the foe;
Where the old trade's plyin' an' the old flag flyin'
   They shall find him ware an' wakin', as they found him long ago.

DRAKE'S DRUM

This is on display at Buckland Abbey, about ten miles north of Plymouth, and is said to have accompanied Drake on many of his adventures. It is a side or snare drum, 21 inches high, made of a barrel of walnut, a type used by foot regiments during the sixteenth century. On one side is painted Drake's heraldic achievement when he was knighted.

Legends have persisted about Drake himself and this famous drum evoking Sir Henry Newbolt to pen the now almost equally well-known lines on this page. It is said that a roll could be heard on this drum when England was in danger from attack.

Drake's flagstaff halfway along Royal Parade marks the re-building of the devastated city during the last world war.

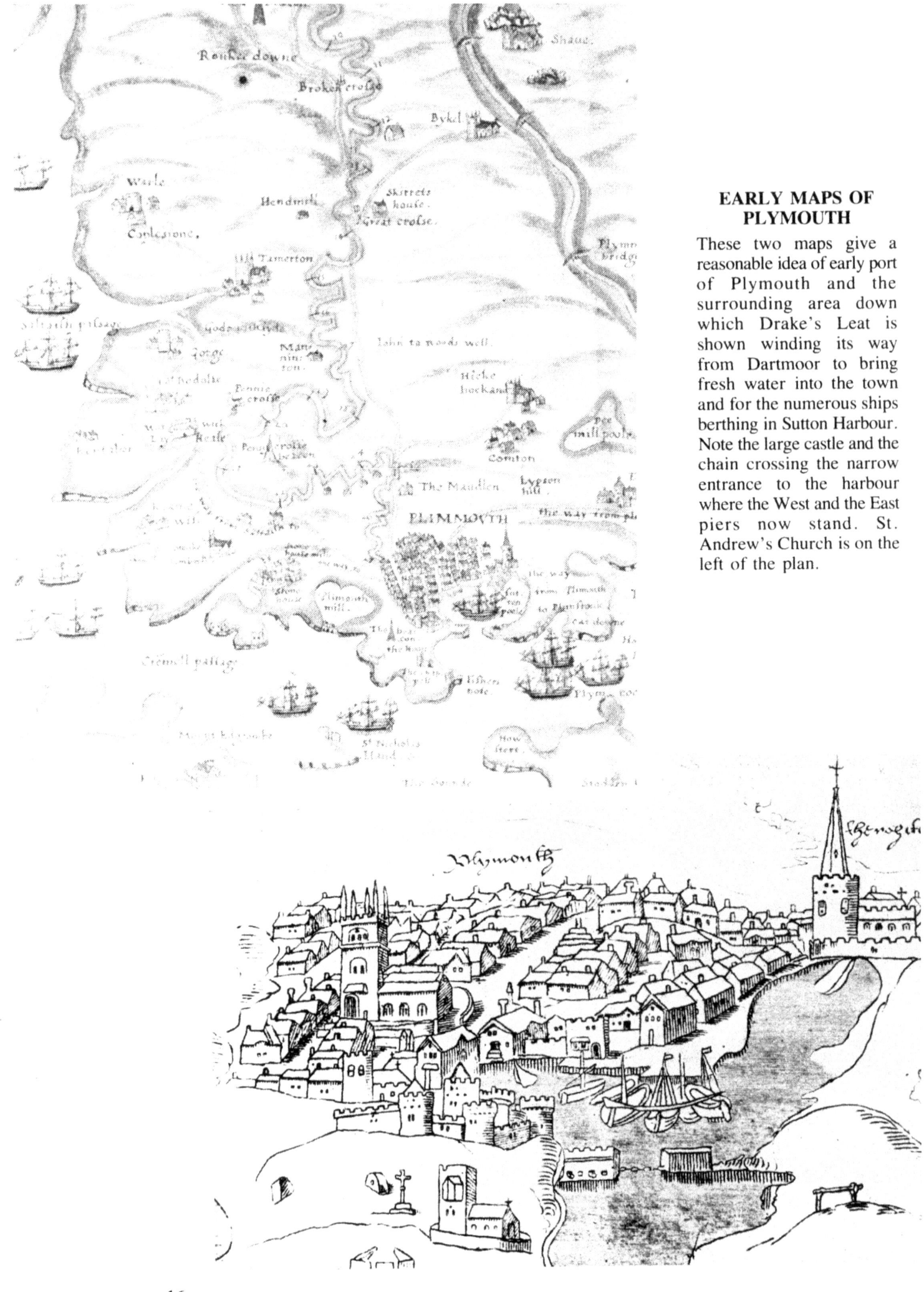

EARLY MAPS OF PLYMOUTH

These two maps give a reasonable idea of early port of Plymouth and the surrounding area down which Drake's Leat is shown winding its way from Dartmoor to bring fresh water into the town and for the numerous ships berthing in Sutton Harbour. Note the large castle and the chain crossing the narrow entrance to the harbour where the West and the East piers now stand. St. Andrew's Church is on the left of the plan.

The Pilgrim Fathers
and
the Mayflower Ship, 1620

Arthur L. Clamp

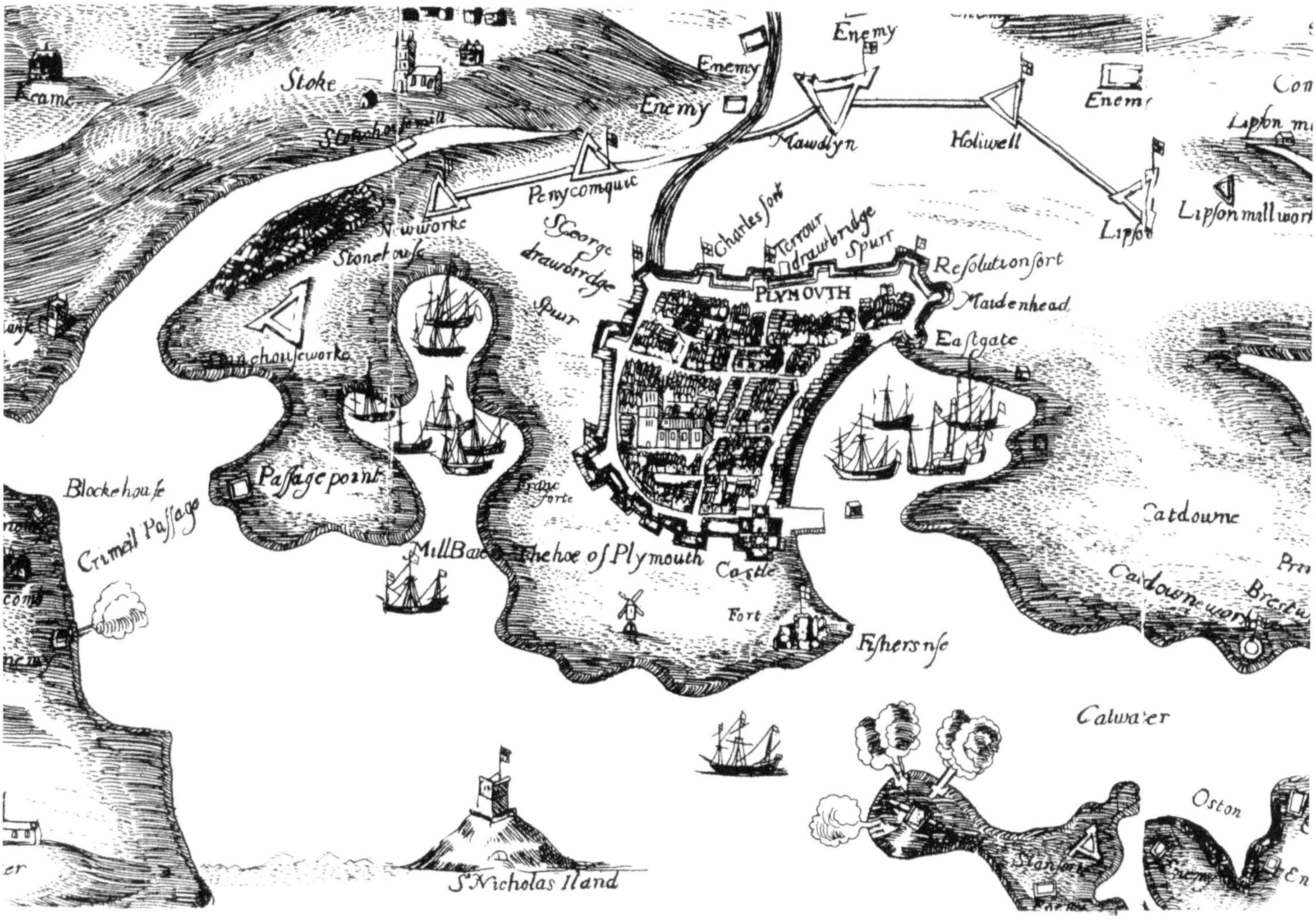

THE TOWN IN THE 1640s

This map of the small port and town of Plymouth shows the walls and fortifications and Sutton Harbour about twenty-five years after the Pilgrims left. The town must have looked very much like this when their ship was moored somewhere between the harbour and Fisher's Nose.

THE PILGRIM FATHERS AND THEIR CAUSE

This historic voyage from the old port of Plymouth in 1620 in a small sailing ship, the *Mayflower*, is perhaps one of the few dates that remain in the memory of most people years after they have left school. It certainly marks a great step forward in the occupation by Europeans of a new land which has grown to be the most powerful nation in the world today.

The journey was not undertaken on an impulse decision but was the culmination of a group of peoples' planning and aspiration towards a way of life and a belief in how God should be worshipped. Its roots go back some forty years before 1620 and draws people from many parts of England and later from where they were living in Holland.

Elizabethan England was adventurous, prosperous and self-assertive in many ways including that of studying the bible in a more direct and understanding manner than was the practice of hearing it being read in churches. It resulted in bringing family and friends together, the saying of family prayers and a new form of worship. Different people from different parts of the country were pursuing this new approach, at first unbeknown to one another, while still in membership with the Church of England. The new form of worship was encouraged by one or two of the Anglican ministers, one being the Rev. Richard Clyfton in Babworth, Nottinghamshire, from 1586. Many people from the surrounding countryside heard of his new approach among them being William Brewster and William Bradford.

These services were, at first, ignored by the church authorities but, with the growth of them, opposition was voiced in various forms and in 1604 Richard Clyfton was deprived of his living. However, he was not long without a place of worship as the manor farmhouse where William Brewster and his family lived was offered to him. Scrooby Manor became, in effect, one of the first new protestant meeting places.

William Brewster had been to Cambridge where he was attracted by a group of radical scholars concerned with the greater freedom of the individual in the interpretation of the scriptures. He had also been to Holland.

Separatist churches were beginning to be formed in other areas and it was not long before these activities, including those at Scrooby Manor, met with disapproval from the Bishops. Brewster was fined £20, a large sum in those days, while others were sent to prison and some fled in fear of their lives.

It had now become quite clear that to avoid continual persecution another country or place would have to be sought where they could practise their religion without hindrance. They turned to Holland and in 1607 attempted to leave by boat but were betrayed and later imprisoned in Boston goal.

A second attempt was successful and many left this part of England for Amsterdam where they met up with other English people from London of a similar leaning. There were three groups here who went about their daily business and worshipped each Sunday as they saw fit for about a year. Then the Scrooby group with others moved out to Leyden and founded the Pilgrim Press out of which came their own version of the Ten Commandments, and literature to send back to England to make their cause more known. By this time many persons destined to become famous through the sailing of the *Mayflower* joined the movement while others remained in England in spite of the persecution.

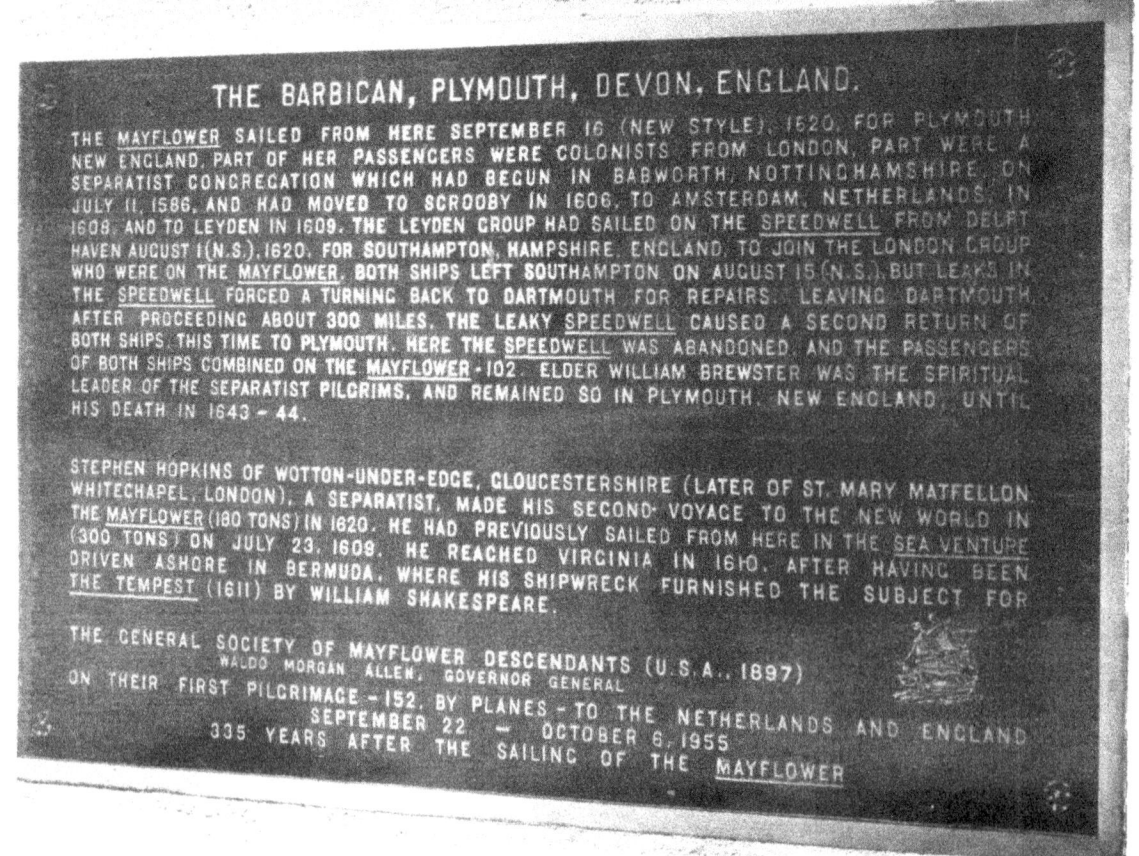

Although they were not in conflict with the local church authorities, the idea of seeking another country was raised as younger members of the group were, as was to be expected, being influenced by local custom and language. It could be that over the years their separate identity and language would be assimilated into the local culture.

Permission was gained from King James I to set up a settlement in the New World and over a period of three years the planned voyage was underwritten by backers to pay for the venture. The *Saints* and the *Strangers*, the adventurers, were the two groups to make up the passengers. The 60 ton vessel, *Speedwell*, was purchased and equipped out and made for Southampton where the *Mayflower* joined her. They left on 15th August, 1620, from the West Quay where there is now a memorial, to start out on the very long crossing.

The *Speedwell*, however, was not up to the journey and sprang a leak forcing both boats into Dartmouth, South Devon, for repairs (see page 14). These were soon attended to and they were sailing again into the Atlantic when out from Land's End the *Speedwell* started to leak again. There was no alternative but to return this time to Plymouth.

They decided to abandon the *Speedwell*. Some disheartened passengers gave up the idea of the crossing and the remainder joined the *Mayflower* with cargo and baggage filling the small ship to its limits. Their stay in Plymouth was very welcomed as the town was sympathetic to their cause.

St. Andrew's Church had a puritan vicar and many of the local people knew about the problems of their crossing and had been to the fishing grounds off the coast of America.

Their stay in the old port was for ten days but they were welcomed and impressed by what was done for them and their departure from Sutton Harbour on 6th September, marked yet another milestone in the maritime story of Plymouth.

PLYMOUTH WELCOMES THE PILGRIMS

In the first account of the journey and the infant colony in 1622, Edward Winslow wrote, *We loosed from Plymouth, having been kindly entertained and courteously used by divers friends there dwelling.* This brief sentence accurately summarises the feelings of the people of Plymouth to the Pilgrims and, in turn, the thoughts of the many persons on the *Mayflower* towards their last port of call.

Their ship, together with the leaking *Speedwell*, would have sailed in close to the Hoe passing Fisher's Nose and probably mooring a little way out from the present west and east piers under the safety of the guns on Plymouth castle, then a large fortification standing on what is now Lambhay Hill. The small port and town (see map on page 1) was largely enclosed by a wall, broken by various gates, and dominated by the square tower of St. Andrew's Church sited about in the centre of the tight-packed houses and narrow streets.

Sutton Harbour was then a little larger than it is today with warehouses and buildings reaching the waterline along the alignment of Quay Road and the old quay line close to the front of island house. The two piers, east and west, were not there but a causey and fish house more or less stood in their place. The facing banks on the Cattedown side were clear of buildings but ships were probably careened and repaired along its shoreline while further in Sutton Harbour around North Quay, houses and other buildings made up the waterfront.

Plymouth, even by 1620, had seen many visitors come and go and fishermen and adventurers from the port knew as much as anyone about the length and hazards of major sea crossing. The economics and trade of the town were closely bound with these activities and with the defence of the realm by the navy who, at this period, were still using this harbour where ships were victualled and prepared for fighting.

This background and style of living had encouraged local people to adopt similar attitudes as the Pilgrims although not so determined as to leave home and all for a new country. However, there was more than general sympathy for the Pilgrims. Plymothians had an independent attitude to authority and the King which came to the fore during their stand for the Parliamentarian cause in the 1640s.

The Pilgrim Fathers could not have picked a better port for help and encouragement in their endeavour to live their lives in a manner they best thought fit. Plymouth had a long Protestant tradition and from about 1608 it was appointing well known puritan preachers and lecturers to St. Andrews and other places of worship. There was a strong protest over vicars being removed from their livings because they were not conforming to the book of Common Prayer. The local Member of Parliament for the town during these years was instrumental in smuggling in leaflets condemning these removals!

There was widespread sympathy for the Puritan causes in town and neighbouring countryside which added to the feelings the local people had towards the Pilgrim Fathers. This background and the port facilities and help given to the ship's passengers by way of food, accommodation and being allowed to worship in the town's main church, was finally and suitably appraised by the Edward Winslow a year later when he had settled with others in the New World.

EXTRACTS FROM THE LOG OF THE MAYFLOWER

It is an almost universal custom for ships to keep logs or records of their progress and ports of call, etc. A log was kept for the *Mayflower* which is one of the few original sources of information on the passage of the two ships along the coast of Devon, the start of their crossing of the Atlantic, the return to Plymouth because of the condition of the *Speedwell*, the transfer of passengers from the *Speedwell* to the *Mayflower* and the final departure of this small ship on its historic journey to the New World.

Tuesday, 22 Sept: Lying at Anchor, Dartmouth Harbour. Both ships ready for sea.

Wednesday, 23 Sept: Weighed anchor, as did consort. Laid course W.S.W. Ships in company. Wind fair.

Thursday, Aug. 24 Sept: Comes in with wind fair. General course W.S.W. Consort in company.

Friday, Aug. 25 Sept: Comes in with wind fair. Course W.S.W. *Speedwell* in company.

Saturday, Aug. 26 Sept: Observations showed ship above 100 leagues W.S.W. of Land's End. *Speedwell* signalled and hove to. Reported leaking dangerously. On consultation between Masters and carpenters of both ships, it was concluded to put back into Plymouth. Bore up for Plymouth. Consort in company.

Sunday, Aug. 27 Sept: Ship on course for Plymouth. *Speedwell* in company.

Monday, Aug. 28 Sept: Made Plymouth harbour, and came to anchor in the Cattewater, followed by consort.

Tuesday, Aug. 29 Sept: At anchor in roadstead. At conference of officers of ship and consort and the chief of the Planter, it was decided to send the *Speedwell* back to London with some 18 or 20 of her passengers, transferring a dozen or more, with part of her lading to the *Mayflower*.

Wednesday, Aug. 30 Sept: At anchor in Plymouth roadstead off the Barbican. Transferring passengers and lading from consort, lying near by. Weather fine.

Thursday, Aug. 31 Sept: At anchor in Plymouth roadstead. Transferring cargo from *Speedwell*.

Friday 1 Sept: At anchor in Plymouth roadstead. Transferring passengers and freight to and from consort. Master Cushman and family, Master Blossom and son, William King, and others with children, going back to London in *Speedwell*. All of *Speedwell*'s passengers who are to make the voyage now aboard. New "governour" of ship and assistants chosen. Master Carver "governour".

Saturday, 2 Sept: At anchor, Plymouth roadstead. Some of principal passengers entertained ashore by friends of their faith. *Speedwell* sailed for London. Quarters assigned, etc.

Sunday, 3 Sept: At anchor in Plymouth roadstead.

Monday, 4 Sept: At anchor in Plymouth roadstead. Some of company ashore.

Tuesday, 5 Sept: At anchor in Plymouth roadstead. Ready for sea.

Wednesday, 6 Sept: Weighed anchor. Wind E.N.E., a fine gale. Laid course W.S.W. for northern coasts of Virginia.

Thursday, 7 Sept: Comes in with wind E.N.E. Light gale continues. Made all sail on ship.

Friday, 8 Sept: Comes in with wind E.N.E. Gale continues. All sails full.

Saturday, 9 Sept: Comes in with wind E.N.E. Gale holds. Ship well off the land.

Sunday, 10 Sept: Comes in with wind E.N.E. Gale holds. Distance lost, when ship bore up for Plymouth, more than regained.

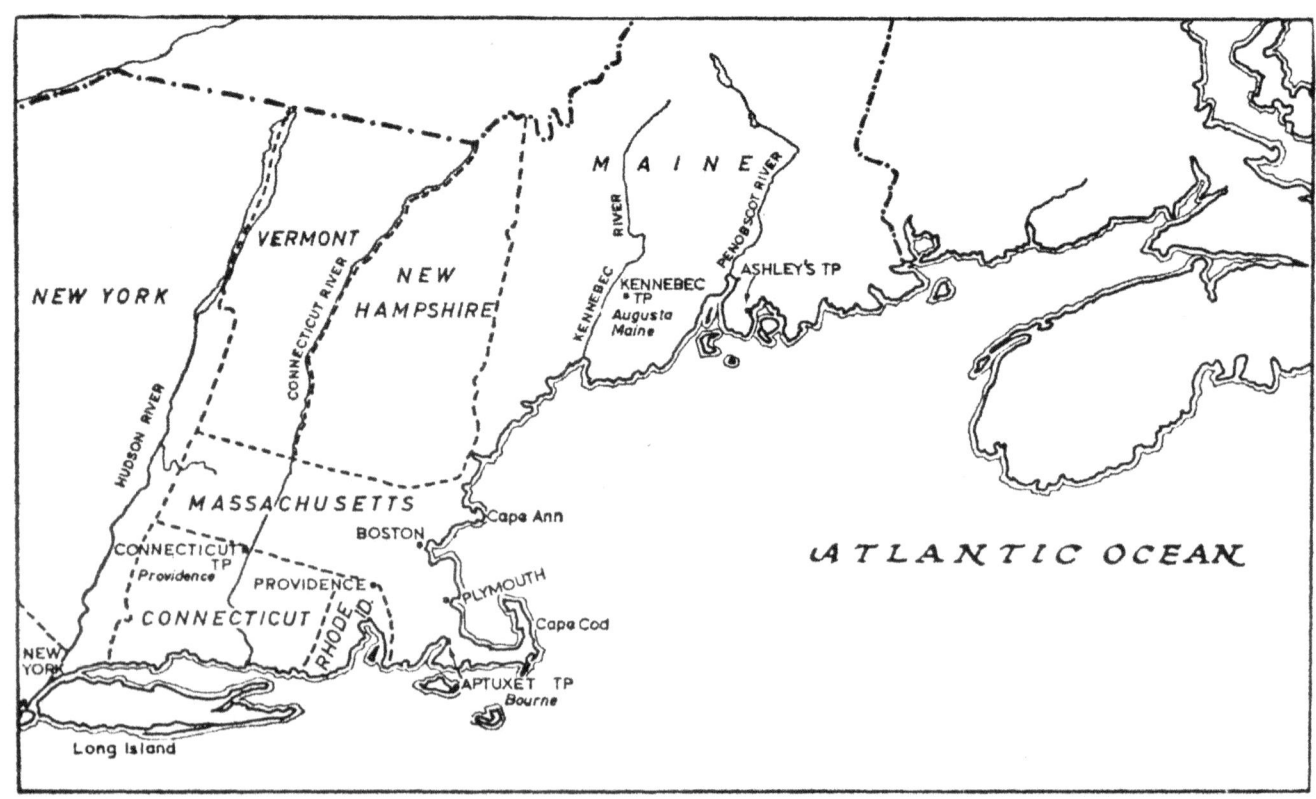

THE MAYFLOWER SHIP AND SHALLOP

An artist's drawing of this famous ship gives a good idea of the general appearance of the vessel and how the passengers and cargo were accommodated above and below the decks. It is thought she was about 200 tons net, 104 ft. long and 25 ft. in width. It is quite clear that quarters were cramped and that the long sea voyage was made more difficult by these conditions. It was necessary to use a shallow draught boat for exploring the coast and inlets of the east coast of the New World and below is a boat very similar to the one used by the Fathers when they cautiously made their way to the shore seeking a safe haven for the larger ship.

PILGRIM PAGEANTS

On special occasions people take part in various commemorative pageants celebrating the departure of the Protestants with song, services and dressing in contemporary costume. Plays and re-enactments of the Pilgrims walking through the Barbican and leaving from the West Pier also take place. Here two local people admirably display the attire of the period standing in the grounds of the old Palace Court in High Street and a group act out the departure of the Pilgrims in 1920.

PASSENGERS ON THE MAYFLOWER SHIP
(from a contemporary book)

The names of those which came over first, in ye year 1620 and were by the blessing of God the first beginers and (in a sort) the foundation of all the Plantations and Colonies in New-England; and their families.

Mr. John Carver; Kathrine, his wife; Desire Minter; & 2 man-servants, John Howland, Roger Wilder; William Latham, a boy; & a maid servant, & a child yt was put to him, called Jasper More.

Mr. William Brewster; Mary, his wife; with 2 sons, whose names were Love and Wrasling; and a boy was put to him called Richard More; and another of his brothers. The rest of his children were left behind, & came over afterwards.

Mr. Edward Winslow; Elizabeth, his wife; & 2 men servants, caled Georg Sowle and Elias Story; also a little girle was put to him, caled Ellen, the sister of Richard More.

William Bradford, and Dorothy, his wife; having but one child, a sone, left behind, who came afterwards.

Mr. Isaack Allerton, and Mary, his wife; with 3 children, Bartholmew, Remember, & Mary; and a servant boy, John Hooke.

Mr. Samuell Fuller, and a servant, caled William Butten. His wife was behind, & a child, which came afterwards.

John Crakston, and his sone, John Crakston.

Captain Myles Standish, and Rose, his wife.

Mr. Christopher Martin, and his wife, and 2 servants, Salamon Prower and John Langemore.

Mr. William Mullines, and his wife, and 2 children, Joseph & Priscila; and a servant, Robart Carter.

Mr. William White, and Susana, his wife, and one sone, caled Resolved, and one borne a ship-bord, caled Peregriene; & 2 servants, named William Holbeck & Edward Thomson.

Mr. Steven Hopkins, & Elizabeth, his wife, and 2 children, caled Giles, and Constanta, a doughter, both by a former wife; and 2 more by this wife, caled Damaris & Oceanus; the last was born at sea; and 2 servants, called Edward Doty and Edward Litster.

Mr. Richard Warren; but his wife and children were lefte behind, and came afterwards.

John Billinton, and Elen, his wife; and 2 sones, John & Francis.

Edward Tillie, and his wife; and Eelizabeth, their doughter.

Francis Cooke, and his sone John. But his wife & other children came afterwards.

Thomas Rogers, and Joseph, his sone. His other children came afterwards.

Thomas Tinker, and his wife, and a sone.

John Rigdale, and Alice, his wife.

James Chilton, and his wife, and Mary, their doughter. They had an other doughter, yt was married, came afterward.

Edward Fuller, and his wife, and Samuell, their sonne.

John Turner, and 2 sones. He had a doughter came some years after to Salem, wher she is now living.

Francis Eaton, and Sarah, his wife, and Samuell, their sone, a yong child.

Moyses Fletcher, John Goodman, Thomas Williams, Digerie Preist, Edmond Margeson, Peter Browne, Richard Britterige, Richard Clerke, Richard Gardenar, Gilbart Winslow.

John Alden was hired for a cooper, at South-Hampton, wher the ship victuled; and being a hopfull yong man, was much desired, but left to his owne liking to go or stay when he came here; but he stayed, and maryed here.

John Allerton and Thomas Enlish were both hired, the later to goe mr of a shalop here, and ye other was reputed as one of ye company, but was to go back (being a seaman) for the help of others behind. But they both dyed here, before the shipe returned.

There were also other 2 seamen hired to stay a year here in the country, William Trevore, and one Ely. But when their time was out, they both returned.

These, bening aboute a hundred sowls, came over in this first ship; and began this worke, which God of his goodness hath hithertoo blesed; let his holy name have ye praise.

CREW AND OTHER PASSENGERS

There were about 150 people on the *Mayflower* of which about 40 were the crew. There was the captain, 4 mates, 4 quartermasters, a surgeon, carpenter, cooper, cooks, boatswains, gunners and others who were mainly engaged to take the ship to the New World and return. Some of these died on the voyage, others stayed with the settlers and the remainder returned to London. The passengers were divided into *Saints*, who were the Pilgrims, and *Strangers*, who were those interested in the voyage as a commercial venture.

REPLICA OF THE MAYFLOWER SHIP, 1957

Mayflower II is seen here starting out on a commemorate voyage from Plymouth in April, 1957, having followed the route of the Pilgrim Fathers from Southampton to Dartmouth and then to Plymouth, their last port of call before journeying to the New World. The ship is permanently moored close to Plymouth Rock, Massachusetts, U.S.A. where many thousands of people visit her each year.

THE MAYFLOWER STONE

This is one of Plymouth's most famous landmarks standing on the West Pier at the entrance to Sutton Harbour. It commemorates the departure of the gallant Pilgrims in 1620 from a point only a matter of yards from here. The pier was built seventy years after they left and the stone erected in 1934, incorporating the much earlier (1891) granite stone, which is now set in the pavement immediately in front of it. Many thousands of visitors from different parts of the world come here to read the details of this historic voyage on the metal plate set in the wall.

THE ISLAND HOUSE

This merchant's house stands at the entrance to New Street and was built in the 1590s. It faces the old Barbican wharf, built a few years previously, and is reputed to have had associations with the Pilgrim Fathers. They would have certainly seen this house from their ship and passed by it when landing on the nearby quayside. For many years it was a ship-chandler supplying local vessels with a variety of materials and goods in readiness for the sea. The well-known Pilgrim board is fixed to its wall.

THE CASTLE QUADRATE

This single buttress of limestone overlooking the Mayflower Stone is the remaining section of an old defensive castle built in the fourteenth century. It controlled the entrance to Sutton Harbour and would have been seen quite clearly by the Pilgrims from their mooring.

THE WEST PIER

The west and east piers were built during the 1790s to partly enclose Sutton Harbour and give safe anchorage to the sailing ships moored inside. The piers were built through the efforts of a Captain McBride whose name is remembered by the nearby inn. This pier now has many commemorative tablets fixed to it and has become a mecca for visitors seeking information about the many historic voyages that started from Plymouth.

MERCHANT'S HOUSE ST. ANDREW'S STREET

This is the most recently restored merchant house in Plymouth and is now under the care of the City Museum. It is open to visitors and houses a very interesting range of local objects from different periods of Plymouth's history. Built in the sixteenth century, it was the residence of William Parker, Mayor of Plymouth in 1601, and was open to the public in its present form in 1978. It is on one of the direct roads running from the old harbour to St. Andrew's Chuch along which the Pilgrims may well have passed when going to the church or the nearby Prysten House.

MERCHANT'S HOUSE, NEW STREET

This is one of the Elizabethan houses in New Street and has been completely restored and now used as a museum showing various aspects of Plymouth's heritage. New Street was built in the 1580s by John Sparke during the very prosperous Elizabethan years and this fine building, together with others, was built for the successful adventurers of those now long-off days. The fine woodwork, centrepole stair beam, which was a ship's mast, and the close setting of the other contemporary buildings would have been seen by the Pilgrims walking up this cobbled street. It was probably less muddy than the lower Southside Street used for walking up to the old town and mother church.

ST. ANDREW'S CHURCH

This is the mother church of Plymouth and stands at the top of Royal Parade, a limestone building with a square tower set against the modern shops and buildings of post-war Plymouth. It was completely gutted during the last war but has been beautifully restored and well worth a visit. Many voyages of exploration and adventure started here with prayers for a safe journey and, like Drake, Frobisher and others, the Pilgrim Fathers would have come here for service before setting out.

THE PRYSTEN HOUSE

This stands on the south side of St. Andrew's Church and was quite old even by the year 1620. It originally housed the priests of St. Andrews and the canons from Plympton Priory and is one of the few buildings of its kind and date left in the city. The Pilgrims would have probably passed it on their way to church although there is nothing to suggest it had any connection with them.

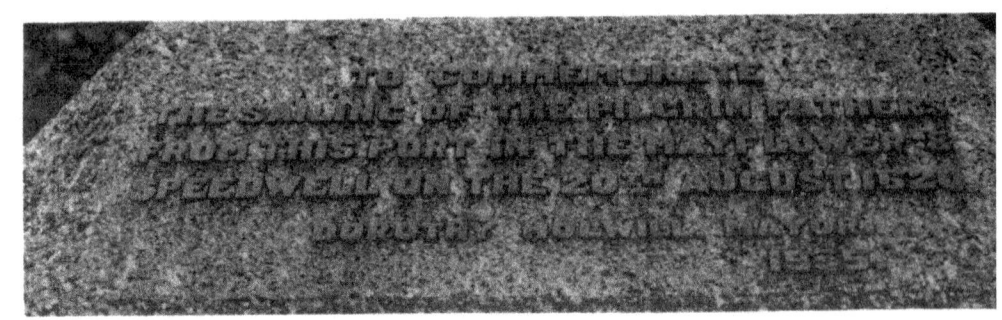

DARTMOUTH

These two plaques give details of the Pilgrim Fathers sailing into the small harbour of Dartmouth when the *Speedwell* sprang a leak. The upper plaque is a commemorative one dated 1955 and the lower was placed here in 1897 by the General Society of Mayflower descendants. The painting depicts the Dartmouth estuary and Baynard's Cove at the time of this historic voyage.

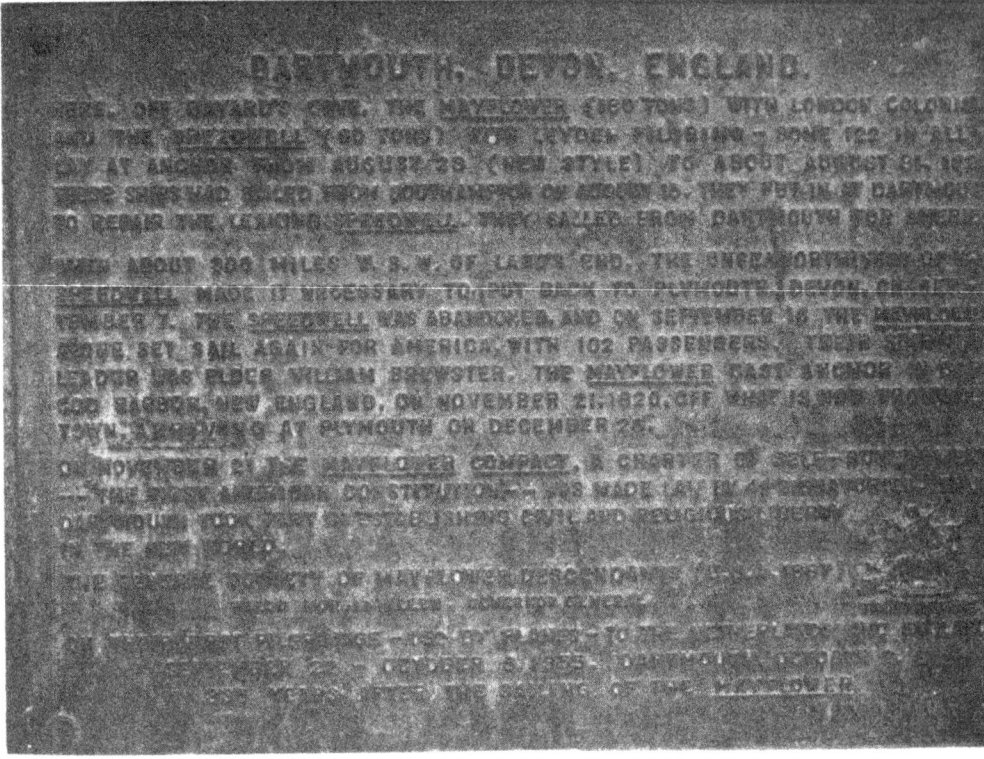

TO THE NEW WORLD

The exact route used by the *Mayflower* is not known but it is thought that it went by the Azores then west to Cape Cod a journey which was logged at sixty-six days. It was certainly not without its hazards as storms and head winds severely shook the small ship and the main beam amid-ship cracked under the strain. She was very heavily loaded and passengers suffered all kinds of discomforts from being wet for most of the time, sea-sick at the outset and with Pilgrims, adventurers and crew all crowded together, conflicts of one kind or another arose. However, in spite of these adverse conditions, Captain Christopher Jones brought the ship to landfall at daybreak on 9th November and only one passenger died *en route*. Elizabeth Hopkins gave birth to a son on board. The delay at Plymouth caused the crossing to be undertaken late in the autumn leaving the settlers to face setting up camp at the start of the winter, not the best time of any year to land on unknown territory.

The *Mayflower* dropped anchor in the lee of Cape Cod, a large headland on the Massachusett's coast just south of Boston. Between early November and 16th December three exploratory journeys were made to find a suitable site for landing goods and passengers and setting up camp. Indians were encountered, and some of the party were almost lost through storms and very bad weather. Finally a safe anchorage within the estuary of the Jones River was found some miles north of the *Mayflower's* first mooring. Here on 16th December the ship dropped anchor and passengers and provisions were taken ashore by the Town Brook on a former Indian site.

The immediate task was to establish defendable living quarters and ferry in as much food and equipment before the onset of winter. Plots were marked out and houses built to hold families or groups of people while others remained on board ship. Plymouth, as the settlement was called, made herculean demands on everyone from working under the most difficult of conditions from early dawn to late evening every day except Sundays. Sickness, in one form or another, was always present and out of about a hundred souls almost fifty had perished by March, 1621.

Contact had been made with the Indians and through being upright and honest in their dealings with them, good relations and co-operation eventually prevailed. The last settlers left the *Mayflower* on 21st March, and on the 5th April, 1621, the ship bade farewell berthing in London a month later.

The first winter brought enormous problems to the infant village but through sheer hard work and a very strong religious belief about half of the Pilgrims survived out of which was born a new nation.

PLYMOUTH ROCK

The engraved date on this "stepping stone" rock records the first landing by one of the Pilgrims at Plymouth in November of that year. Tradition has it that this was the actual rock on the shore which gave firm footing to the first passenger to land. It now forms the centre-piece of a large commemorative shrine and has been suitably described as the *cornerstone of a nation*.

THE SETTLEMENT GROWS

The dreadful first winter passed and the summer months gave them new spirit and opportunity for many schemes of land clearing and planting, building houses and making stronger their first attempts at fortifying the settlement. Houses and gardens were surrounded by heavy wooden fences and a fort, mounted with small cannon, stood above the general level of the buildings which was guarded most of the time. There were problems of sickness and general shortages of food but the abundance of natural food and fish helped them to stave off any calamity.

Their good relations with the indians and their contact with two of its members did bring about benefits for both sides although there were, at times, moments when these did appear to be somewhat frail. Various expeditions to find food, the lay of the land and to bring in supplies were taking place using the shallop to explore the coastline and treking through the scrub and forest inland. Bartering often took place with beads, etc. for skins and food which all helped in establishing the colony and giving confidence to its settlers.

The *Mayflower* had long returned home but ships did appear along the seaboard out from England for fishing and trade with men coming in to visit Plymouth sometimes imposing extra demands upon their meagre supplies and resources. However, by 1623 other settlers were beginning to follow in the Pilgrim's footsteps with authority from the Plymouth Virginia Company to break in land and develop homesteads in many parts of Massachusetts. People came out from Plymouth, Leyden in Holland and other places many of whom knew the first Pilgrims.

The exodus of people determined to practice their faith as they thought best continued throughout the 1620s but thereafter the number of settlers grew to such an extent that a new nation was well on the way to being formed.

AFTER THE VOYAGE

Many paintings show various aspects of the Pilgrims in their homestead. This well-known one shows a family group looking out to sea and probably thinking about the folk they have left behind. Their decision to make a new life in a new land could not be changed yet little did they realise what a great step they were making in pioneering the opening of such a large country to many thousands of settlers over the coming years.

Arthur L. Clamp – the man behind the books

Arthur Leslie Clamp was a man of boundless energy with a passion for helping others, particularly through his love of history. A printer by trade, he started his career in a printing company before moving his family from Exeter to Plymouth to teach at the Plymouth College of Art and Design, where he eventually became the Head of the Printing Department.

A Devoted Family Man

Arthur with his five children.

Despite his love of teaching, Arthur prioritised his family, always making it home by 5:30pm for tea. He and his wife, Rosemary, raised five children: Susan, Angela, Elizabeth, David, and Steven. Arthur would often combine his love of family and history by taking his children on Sunday walks, encouraging them to appreciate historical monuments by taking photos or making crayon rubbings of gravestones for his books. The family home at 203 Elburton Road was a hub of activity, with a large garden, featuring a two-storey fort and a makeshift swimming pool.

A Lifelong Learner and Adventurer

Arthur's thirst for knowledge extended beyond history to a deep curiosity about the world. He was passionate about exploring different cultures, traditions, and cuisines, often taking advantage of his long summer holidays as a teacher to travel to places like India, Russia, South America, the middle east and the USA, sometimes bringing one of his children along. This adventurous spirit even influenced his home life, as seen by the short-lived family tradition of steam-cooking vegetables after a trip to Iceland.

History is a prominent feature of family days out

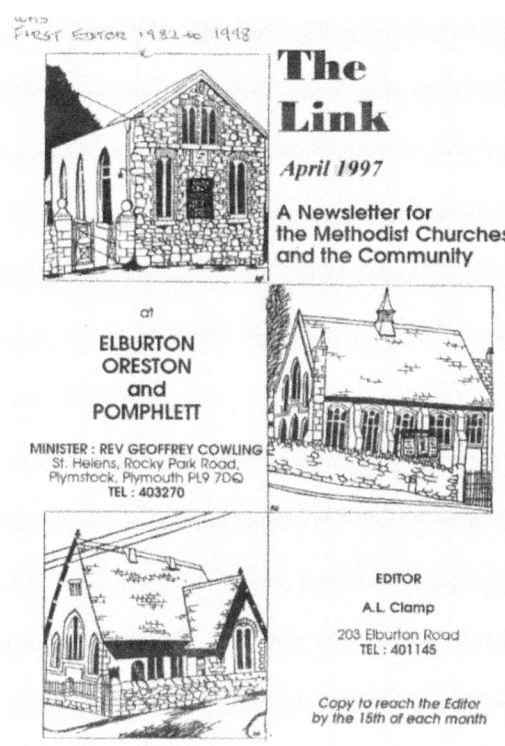

Community and Philanthropic Spirit

His commitment to serving others was evident in his long-standing involvement with the Elburton Methodist Church. He was the Sunday School Superintendent for over 15 years and served as the editor of the wider church's monthly newsletter, "The Link," for a similar duration. After Rosemary's very sad passing, Arthur later remarried and, following a chance encounter with a professor from India, established a connection with a missionary school in Chennai. Together with his new wife, Christine, he co-founded a "Sponsor a Child's Education" program that continues to this day.

Pictured left – The cover of 'The Link' complete with hand drawn sketches of each church by Angela
Below right – Arthur Clamp promoting his latest book
Below left – Arthur at home with his first wife, Rosemary
Below centre – Arthur on holiday with his second wife, Christine

A Legacy of Learning and Positivity

Arthur's greatest passion was history, which he brought to life through tireless research, documentation, and the many books he authored. He was driven by a need to "never be stuck in a rut," constantly seeking new experiences, meeting new people, and expanding his knowledge. With a positive attitude and a great sense of humour, he was always ready to help others, leaving a lasting impact on his family and community. His children, Susan, Angela, Elizabeth, David, and Steven, remember him with love and gratitude.

David Clamp, 2025

A Legacy of Local History

Below is the story of how Arthur L Clamp began writing books, in his own words, drafted shortly before he passed away in 2001. I have only made minor alterations to this text, correcting grammatical errors that he did not survive to correct himself. When I first discovered this text, I was shocked to see my name mentioned. It seems that, unbeknownst to me, I shared my first PC with him. I suspect he used it during the day when I was at school, although I do have one memory of sitting with him and showing him how it worked. It has been a pleasure to pick up where he left off and see his books republished and redistributed, and to know that I was part of the story, even back then. It was also fascinating to discover that his pricing structure matches the way I have tried to price the books, with a third going to local sellers and the rest covering printing costs with a little left over for my expenses.

I am his eldest grandson, and it is a privilege to curate his legacy, which we are calling 'The Clamp Collection'. The very last line of the text originally reads "The following pages list all the titles." Sadly, that page is missing and we have no record of all the books he published and knowing that some of those were researched by other authors makes the process of finding them even harder. I look forward to one day completing the collection and seeing them all available again. And maybe, one day, I'll even start writing my own to add to the series. For now, here is his story in his own words.

Steven Gibson, 2025

Writing and Publishing Booklets on Local Topics and Areas

I started this interest in either 1968 or 1969 when living in Woodford. I had by these dates established the Department of Printing and I think I must have been looking for something different to do. The first titles were of A5 size proofed from type set at Clarke, Doble and Brendon, Ltd., Plymouth printers, and then made up into pages and printed at Sawtell and Neilson, Ltd., Totnes.

Then began a slow process of getting them out to shops, etc. which proved to be more time consuming and difficult than actually researching, writing and getting the books into print. However, I persisted and opened a business account with Barclays Bank on the Broadway. I was advised to give it a title so I called it "Westway Publications". There came along another problem, one of storage of paper and finished books which was solved when the family moved to Elburton in 1970.

I changed the printer to Penwell, Ltd., Callington, Cornwall, as he was then just setting up himself and his prices seemed very reasonable. I did not get any of the printers to make up the complete books. I hand folded the flat printed sheets, stitched the books on a small manual table stitcher and trimmed them in a small hand turned guillotine which I bought from someone in Penzance for £40. It was brought up in a van.

The trouble and time going to and fro to Callington was too much so I transferred the printing to PDS Printers, Prince Rock, Plymouth, and I have been with them ever since. Now they are at Plympton which is easy to reach and they fold the flat sheets which was turning out to be a long chore which only saved a small part of the printing costs.

All my first titles were written by myself. I took the photographs and developed them in the loft of the house, the type was set by now on a computer situated in the house at Elburton from which I had collected photographic lengths of text to cut up and law down as pages.

At some point I decided that I would do my own film processing of lith film so I bought a large second hand process camera from Kingsbridge and learnt through trial and error to make line negatives of the text and halftone negatives of the illustrations which proved more difficult than I anticipated. The main problem was trying to keep the developer in the large dish at the correct temperature as any change would affect the developing time. I replaced this old camera with a brand new one bought from Croydon, Surrey, costing £900. This has turned out to be a great asset cutting out an expensive part of the printer's costs and one crucial aspect of the work which I could control.

By the middle 1970s there were many outlets I had contacted in Plymouth, up to Dartmoor, Exeter, around to Torbay, Totnes, Dartmouth and the South Hams. The market for local books was much greater than I had first thought and through getting to know many local people undertaking research themselves had the chance to help and make up books for other people who had in most instances, got together a collection of photographs with some text in a rather muddled way. Through my experience in print I was able to shape up their work and get it into print and in every case I had to pay the printer and let the person have the royalties. In the majority of titles produced in this manner this was another way of producing titles and it did give some profit to my work. However, I must say that in a few cases I lost out by either the other person getting the numbers wrong, not returning any monies from stock I delivered or they thought that more of their books should have been sold.

The print run was usually 1,000 copies and from time to time I have had reprints of 250 copies. It took about ten years to clear the first print run so I always had large stocks in the garage, workshop, etc. The numbers sold during the early years was about 7,000 copies a year increasing to around 9,000 copies and for the whole of the enterprise about 500,000 have been sold. The booklets have become part of the local scene and many people collect them, shops regularly order copies and I go around certain areas month by month restocking or replacing titles as necessary.

During the past year or so I have started setting the text on a Packard Bell PC, something which I should have done some years back. I share it with Steven Gibson, my grandson. There appears to be no end to the market for local books, but I could not earn a regular income because of the long time it takes to sell stock.

However, now exceeding 100 titles made up mainly of A4 twenty-four page booklets, some folded guides, with selling prices set with a third going to the shop which is the trade custom, the original idea has been quite successful and could go on for ever.

Apart from monetary benefits, however spasmodically these might be, I have learnt a lot myself, met many interesting people and have become part of the local scene with requests to give talks and to advise people about getting into print.

Arthur L Clamp, 2001

Death of local historical author

'He was an incredible character who was just loved by everybody who knew him'

A WELL-loved Elburton author has died at the age of 68.

Arthur Clamp (pictured right), who was one of the West Country's most successful writers, died at St Luke's Hospice, Turnchapel, after losing his battle against cancer.

Tributes have been flooding in for a man who was known in the community as a prominent writer and outgoing person.

He produced more than 140 titles during his life, dealing with both fiction, fact and history, often discussing West Country topics that were close to his heart.

One of his most acclaimed books was *The Plymouth Blitz*, and he also won credit for *The Rise and Fall of the Bearings of Membland Hall*, set in Noss Mayo.

He achieved sales of between 7,000 and 9,000 books every year and it is estimated that he has sold over half a million books, covering the areas of Plymouth, Dartmoor, Exeter, Torbay and the South Hams.

Mr Clamp was born in Mitcham, Surrey, in 1932, and was the eldest of four children.

He moved to Devon in 1941 to avoid the London air-raids.

Mr Clamp trained as a printer in Exeter and also gained a teachers' certificate in 1959 from Garnet College in London.

Plymouth College of Art, however, was to prove to be Mr Clamp's working home for the following 32 years until 1991, when he retired as head of the printing department.

He had a great interest in travel and had visited the USA, Tanzania, China, Russia, Peru, as well as travelling across Europe, where he presented talks and slide shows on his experiences as a writer.

Mr Clamp was a member of Elburton Methodist Church for many years, superintendent of the Sunday school and editor of the church newsletter, as well as being involved in much charity work.

He was president of the Plymouth and District Field Club and an active member of the Elburton Residents' Association.

He enjoyed leading walks on Dartmoor and historical tours throughout the West Country.

Mr Clamp married his first wife, Rosemary, in 1956 and they had five children – Susan, Angela, Elizabeth, David and Steven – and she died in 1987. He also had 11 grandchildren.

He leaves a wife Christine, after remarrying in 1991, and her two children and three grandchildren.

'He was an incredible character who was just loved by everybody who knew him,' said his wife.

'He will be missed by his family, his friends, the people he worked with and just everybody who knew him through his books.'

More than 300 mourners attended his funeral at Elburton Methodist Church on Monday.

'The attendance was a celebration of his life – he would have found that really special. It shows his vibrancy and love of people,' said Mrs Clamp.

Steven Clamp added that his father was 'a well respected and loved man, missed by a great many people throughout the South West and far beyond'.

This newspaper article, published by the Evening Herald on 17th August 2001, forms a good record of his life. Just as he encourages us to learn more about local history, we encourage you to learn a little about him. For that reason, we have included these pages at the back of all the most recently republished books, in honour of his memory and recognition of his contribution to the community.

www.ingramcontent.com/pod-product-compliance
Lightning Source LLC
Chambersburg PA
CBHW061405070526
44584CB00031B/4164